jx
340
BAK

Baker, Eugene
    I want to be a lawyer; illustrated by Phil Kantz. Childrens Press, 1973.
    31p. illus.

DISCARDED BY
DELPHI PUBLIC LIBRARY

The duties and training of a lawyer.

1 Law as a profession   I Title   340

Associated Libraries, Inc.

I want to be a
LAWYER

By Eugene Baker
Illustrated by Phil Kantz

COUNTY LINE CHURCH OF GOD
LIBRARY
R. R. 2
AUBURN, INDIANA 46706

CHILDRENS PRESS, CHICAGO

Library of Congress Cataloging in Publication Data

Baker, Eugene H
 I want to be a lawyer.

 SUMMARY: Easy-to-read text describes a lawyer's job and training.
 1. Law as a profession—United States—Juvenile literature. (1. Law as a profession) I. Kantz, Phil, illus. II. Title.
KF297.Z9B28   340'.023   73-771
ISBN 0-516-01744-0

Copyright© 1973 by Regensteiner Publishing Enterprises, Inc.
All rights reserved. Published simultaneously in Canada
Printed in the United States of America.

1 2 3 4 5 6 7 8 9 10 11 12 13 14 15 16 17 18 19 20 21 22 23 24 25 R 75 74 73

"They're here," Brian called. He grabbed his football and ran out.

"Hi Paul! Welcome home," Brian shouted. "Go out for a long pass." They played until lunchtime.

"What do you do at college?" asked Brian as they sat down.

"I'm studying to be a lawyer," Paul answered.

"Like Dad?"

"Yes. You know that a lawyer is also called an attorney. He helps people know their legal rights. He tells them the rights they have under the law. Sometimes a lawyer talks for people in court."

About the author:
Dr. Baker was graduated from Carthage College, Carthage, Illinois. He got his master's degree and doctorate in education at Northwestern University. He has worked as a teacher, as a principal, and as a director of curriculum and instruction. Now he works full time as curriculum consultant. His practical help to schools where new programs are evolving is sparked with his boundless enthusiasm. He likes to see social studies and language arts taught with countless resources and many books to encourage students to think independently, creatively, and critically. The Bakers, who live in Arlington Heights, Illinois, have a son and two daughters.

About the Artist:
Phil Kantz is a graphic designer for advertising and publishing. He holds degrees from the University of Illinois and the Chicago Academy of Fine Arts. Recently, Phil won first place in the Christmas Seal designs. He exhibits regularly at the Artists Guild of Chicago and presently lives in Skokie, Illinois, with his wife and two daughters.

"It's close to the court buildings. Look down the street. That is the state courthouse."

"When I finish law school I will work in that building," remarked Paul.

"Maybe I will too," added Brian.

"We'll see," smiled dad.

Two weeks later, the family was driving to the airport. Paul's vacation was over.

"Brian, look to your right," dad said. "That is where I work. Many lawyers have offices here."

"Why?" asked Brian.

"Well it is," answered mother, "but it's worth it. America is independent today because men, some of them lawyers, thought the rights of the people were more important than those of a faraway king. Men of law have never stopped trying to see that people are treated justly."

"Then," Paul said, "I will work with dad or other lawyers. At first I will do simple work—filling out forms and looking up past cases for older lawyers. After awhile I will handle my own cases."

"It sure sounds like a lot of work," Brian said.

"What will Paul do when he finishes law school?" asked Brian.

"First, he must take a test and get his license. This is called being admitted to the bar in our state," answered dad.

"After years of hard work, some lawyers become judges," dad said. "The judge must be very fair and know the law. He or she is the one who hears both sides of the legal argument. Often the judge must decide what the law says and which side wins the case."

"A lawyer must also know how to get along with people. This is important. A lawyer spends much of his time talking with people who have problems," said Paul.

"There's a lot to learn," added dad. "Much of the law is based on older court decisions. That is why a law library is so important. The law books contain past cases, legal agreements, and all the laws that protect property and individuals."

"I didn't know that!" Brian exclaimed. "How long do you have to go to school to be a lawyer?"

Paul laughed. "Longer than you think. After I finish college I must go to law school for three years."

"Many lawyers work for the government," answered dad. "Some of the presidents of the United States have been lawyers. Other lawyers work in banks and large businesses."

"Like lawyers I see on TV?" asked Brian.

"Yes and no," Paul answered. "Those lawyers usually are helping people accused of a crime. That is only one part of a lawyer's job."